D1190066

The Musubi Man

Hawai'i's Gingerbread Man

Sandi Takayama

Illustrated by Pat Hall

The Bess Press
3565 Harding Avenue
Honolulu, Hawai'i 96816

Cover design: Paula Newcomb

Once upon a time in a tiny house in the middle of a taro patch there lived a little old woman and a little old man. They worked hard all day tending to their taro.

Early every morning the little old woman made nourishing meals for their lunch and dinner. Her meals were most delicious and they were always made of rice—sushi rice, fried rice, fish with rice . . . rice, rice, rice!

One morning the little old woman wanted to make something different. She thought and thought and then she smiled. "I know," she said. "I'll make a musubi man."

And so she did.

She gave him limu hair and a little nori jacket, two takuan eyes, an ebi nose, and a smiling mouth of red ginger. "He needs something else to make him extra special. Perhaps an umeboshi would do the trick." When she reached into the ume jar, she pulled out an umeboshi in the shape of a heart.

"Ah, perfect!" exclaimed the little old woman. And she placed the umeboshi heart on the musubi man right where a heart should be.

As soon as the umeboshi heart was in place, the musubi man winked one yellow takuan eye at the little old woman and sat up. He hopped off the table, ran across the kitchen floor, and pushed open the screen door.

"Stop!" yelled the little old woman, running as fast as she could.

"Stop! Stop!" yelled the little old man, as the musubi man ran through the taro patch.

But the runaway musubi man just laughed. "Run, run, fast as you can! You no can catch me, I'm one musubi man!" And he ran down the dirt road.

The little old woman and the little old man ran right after him.

The musubi man ran past a big poi dog gnawing on a bone. "Stop!" barked the poi dog, dropping the bone and running after the musubi man.

But the musubi man only laughed. "Run, run, fast as you can! You no can catch me, I'm one musubi man! I wen' run away from one little old woman and one little old man, and I going run away from you, too, I can, I can."

And he could!
Because the little old woman and the little old man and the poi dog just could not catch him.

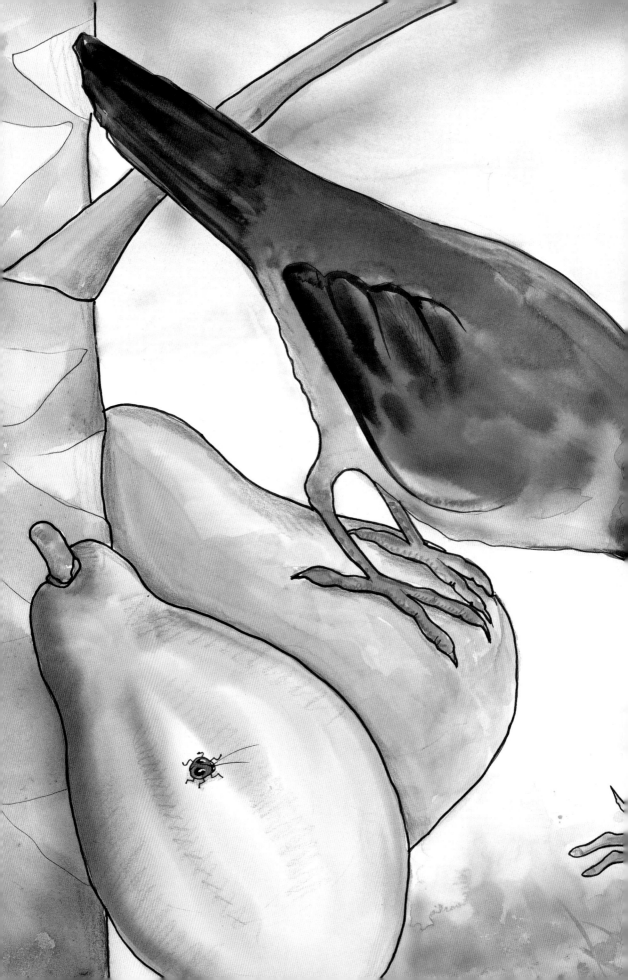

Next, the musubi man passed a noisy mynah bird sitting up high in a papaya tree. "Stop! Stop! Stop right now!" screeched the noisy mynah bird.

The musubi man laughed and laughed. "Run, run, fast as you can! You no can catch me, I'm one musubi man! I wen' run away from one little old woman and one little old man and one big poi dog, and I going run away from you, too, I can, I can."

And on ran the musubi man.

On ran the little old woman, the little old man, the big poi dog and the noisy mynah bird.

Soon the musubi man passed a sleek mongoose sunning himself on a rock. "Stop! Stop! Stop!" chittered the mongoose. But the musubi man laughed at the mongoose.

"Run, run, fast as you can! You no can catch me, I'm one musubi man! I wen' run away from one little old woman and one little old man and one big poi dog and one noisy mynah bird, too. No way I going stop for you!" And he ran on and on.

And so did the little old woman, the little old man, the big poi dog, the noisy mynah bird and the sleek mongoose. But they were all getting very, very tired.

Suddenly, the musubi man came to a beach. He ran across the sand and reached the ocean. There was no way for him to cross it.

Just then a surfer appeared. "Hop onto my back, musubi man. I'll take you across the ocean." The surfer smiled, and his white teeth glowed in his tanned face.

The musubi man noticed those teeth. He did not hop on the surfer's back. Instead, he climbed onto the very edge of the surfboard, and the surfer paddled out.

As the wave came closer and closer, the water splashed farther and farther along the surfboard and the musubi man moved a little closer to the surfer.

"C'mon, musubi man, hop onto my back or you'll get soaked." The musubi man took another look at the waves and hopped onto the surfer's back.

The waves splashed higher and higher and nearly covered the surfer's back. "You'd better hop onto my head, musubi man," called the surfer. "Unless you want to be rice soup." The musubi man hopped onto the surfer's head.

The wave grew larger and larger. "Hey, you'd better get into my mouth. It's the only safe place to be."

The musubi man looked at the surfer's mouth and looked at the huge wave. What should he do? He decided to jump, but before he could do it the wave was upon them. He and the surfer rode it all the way through the barrel and back to the shore.

"Wow! That was the best ride I ever had! You must be good luck, little musubi man. Sorry about trying to eat you. Want to catch another wave?"

"Surf, surf, fast as you can, you can catch any wave with the musubi man!" replied the musubi man. And they were off. They caught wave after wave the entire day.

The surfer eventually turned pro and went on to win many international meets. And always on his shoulder was the little musubi man.

As for the little old woman, she didn't keep up with the surfing world and so she always wondered what happened to her runaway musubi man. She often thought about making another musubi man, but neither she nor anyone else has ever been able to find another heart-shaped umeboshi.

Glossary

ebi	dried shrimp
limu	seaweed
musubi	cooked rice usually shaped into triangles or balls. Sometimes an umeboshi is placed in the middle.
nori	sheets of dried seaweed
barrel	surfing term for a wave that curls to form a tube.
poi dog	mixed-breed dog
sushi	rice seasoned with vinegar sauce
takuan	pickled radish
taro	a plant with a starchy root that is pounded to make poi. The leaves can be used to wrap steamed foods.
umeboshi (ume)	Japanese plum, soaked in brine and packed with red shiso (beefsteak or perilla) leaves